MONITOR

In the same series

Animal Soup

MONITOR

A Screenplay by David V G Davies

Based on the story by David V G Davies

with additional material by
Lee O'Neill and Peter Kinman

released through

From the Shadows Ltd

Published in 2016
by From the Shadows Limited

© 2011 From The Shadows Limited
introduction © 2016 From The Shadows Limited

Printed by Createspace

For 'Goblin' Pete

CONTENTS

Introduction
ix

Original Synopsis
xi

Cold Harbour:
First Synopsis 2008
xii

Alice:
Rewrite Synopsis 2009
xiv

Monitor
Final Synopsis 2009
xvi

Monitor
Final Shooting Script
1

INTRODUCTION

Monitor began life on paper as a proposed sequel to Animal Soup, a film I helped bring to the screen. That film's success made myself and co creator JAK look at the possibilities of exploring the characters more. After a year of writing we both decided that due to independent films rarely having a successful sequel that we would work our ideas in to a companion film so that watching Animal Soup wasn't necessarily needed. JAK decided to develop a story centring on two characters that were cut from the final film while I decided to look at the possibilities of a prequel where the antagonists of the first film were incarcerated at a facility and the story of their escape would unfold.

During numerous rewrites and my passion for the stories of Lewis Carroll my story developed in to one of a girl who accidentally stumbles upon this hidden facility and gets mistaken as one of the patients, her struggle to escape forming the basis or the plot.

Wanting to learn more about the film making process but again on such a micro budget was proving difficult and certain script elements did sadly not make it to the final cut. I wanted to learn compositing and visual effect and in particular learn the Adobe After Effects software, something that looked and sounded very alien to me. Elements of computer graphics were written in to the script and the entity of an all seeing eye was created allowing for digital effects to become a character within the story allowing for my own development to occur.

Employing likeminded cast and crew who also wanted a project to serve as a learning curve production began in early 2010 in Essex and continued over a 6 month period. We did over run and I did over spend but this film did teach me that I couldn't multi task some of the roles needed. Since this film I have made a point of employing assistant directors, continuity and runners as these roles certainly are essential to any films success.

Sadly during the production, a close friend of mine and valued crew member on this project passed away and led to my shelving of this project for some time. The encouragement from family, friends and fans helped us finish this film without him. He will always be missed and I know he would be glad the film is finished although he no doubt will complain that some scenes are not to his standard and we did have to cut out several effects based scenes.

This book contains the final shooting script as the film was intended. Sadly some scenes were altered and others cut completely but I hope you enjoy it as much as I enjoyed envisioning it. Included as a bonus are the original synopsis' written in 2008 so you can see how the story changed over the course of writing.

Monitor served as a great learning curve to me and elements of its story have continued to appear in my latter work.

Many thanks and I hope you enjoy.

David V G Davies

Early Script Synopsis

The following three synopsis are taken from various points in the rewriting process of Monitor, Some key elements stayed and others were removed. The progress of rewrites certainly changed during the two year development period of this script.

Cold Harbour:
First draft Synopsis 2008

This First draft script synopsis would serve as a prequel to Animal Soup and deal with the first stage in the origins of that film's antagonists.

COLD HARBOUR

Alice is a extreme adrenaline junkie and during an off road mountain bike trek her bike chain slips causing her to fall. While repairing her bike she notices a man crawl under a chain fence and catch a rabbit with his bare hands, he kills it and as she tries to get to her feet and peddle off she turns in to a second man, a man wearing a surgical mask covered in blood, he hits her over the head with a leg bone and drags her back under the fence. Along with the rabbit killing man.

Alice awakes in a mental health facility, not knowing how she got there or anything about her past she befriends a simple minded janitor and convinces him to help her escape. An all seeing cctv program monitors everything and the orderlies of the facility try to put an end to their hi-jinx. The mask wearing man and rabbit killer, turn out to be patients as well and have been planing their own uprising, they go on a killing spree offing everyone apart from Alice who they beat severely leaving her brain damaged, they burn the facility to the ground, escaping to the wilderness dragging Alice with them to become the mother of their children.

The closing sequence of the film is her giving birth to a deformed offspring.

Alice
Rewrite synopsis 2009

Elements from the previous synopsis remained but more character development was placed upon the Character Alice who was our door way to this pre-existing world. Ties to Animal soup were lost and the film dropped more references to Alice in Wonderland and the character of a sinister all seeing mastermind was developed.

ALICE

Sarah is doing coke in her bathroom, her husband George, returns home and an argument between them ensues leading to her running away and turning to prostitution to feed her habit. George not willing to let go starts searching for her.

Sarah, while intoxicated gets in to the car of Hooper, he decides to take her to his workplace to become part of his therapy program where he and other orderlies of the Vernon Institute take out their frustration upon waifs and strays. On his drive to work he accidentally knocks down a cyclist, Alice. Seeing that she is still alive he bundles her in to the car as well and takes them both to work,

The janitor of the Vernon institute witnesses the arrival of these two unconscious victims and decides to take a stand, he recognises Sarah from missing posters and gets in touch with George, they begin a plan to get proof before contacting the authorities.
The find Alice who tells them of the fate of Sarah, she has been beaten and raped to death, her body is ready to be incinerated within the basement maze of rooms.

George, in a fit of rage, lashes out and in the gets killed, Alice becomes free and makes a run for it, setting a fire during her escape that escalates in to a gas explosion. She crawls through the rubble and under a fence, but she trips when startled by a security dog and rolls down the hill on to the dual carriageway and gets hit by a car.

The Vernon Institute mastermind watched it all unfold on cctv, deletes the footage, shreds his folder named Transfer program and then starts working on one called Reassignment.

Monitor
Synopsis 2010

In this script rewrite with additional material from Lee O'Nell and Peter Kinman, the presence of the CCTV cameras took on a character trait , which helped with my goal of leading software. Certain back stories were removed and the character of Alice was developed more and she became the focal point of the story. The Bleak ending was kept and allowed for this to be a stand alone film with an obvious beginning and an ending that would be controversial.

MONITOR

Alice is a young offender, her pyromaniac tendencies led to her parents death, due to her age she is placed under the care of the Damocles Foundation.

The staff of the Damocles foundation have developed a therapy session where they abuse the patients with no next of kin, Alice just so happen to be their next target but her friendship with the newly appointed Janitor has led to a spanner in the works.

The devious Orderlies take matters up a notch and kill George and take Alice to the basement with the intention of increasing their therapy sessions no longer under the watchful eye of the CCTV (Is it the facility manager or some other global dominating character). Alice breaks free as the orderlies own troubles get the better of them, she sets the building on fire to cover her tracks and escapes in the confusion only to be stopped in her tracks by an accident.

The all seeing eye, covers up all the malpractice and initiates another sinister therapy session for her staff in on the other side of the world at one of many facilities.

MONITOR
The Shooting Script

MONITOR was released worldwide in 2015. the cast and crew includes

ALICE	Yana Kolesnyk
HOOPER	Rami Hilmi
CARPENTER	Emily Wicket
BARKER	Janine
GEORGE	JD Gillam
CHERYL	Jennifer Bright
NURSE RATCHED	Victoria Broom
NURSE PRICE	Dani Thompson
STABBY JOE	Peter Kinman
PROFESSOR DAMOCLES	Antony Barden
NEWSCASTER	Eleanor James
SAFFRON DAMOCLES	Suzi Lorraine
Director	David V G Davies
Producers	David V G Davies
	Yana Kolesnyk
	Peter Kinman
Screenplay	David V G Davies
Cinematography	Francesco Bartiromo
Special Effects	Peter Kinman
	Kelly Proto
Production Design	David V G Davies
Music	Chris J Nairn
Editor	David V G Davies

EXT. DAMOCLES FOUNDATION - TV INFOMERCIAL

Establishing shot of an ageing building. Cut with flower beds and pleasant scenes of autumn.
PROFESSOR DAMOCLES *is in his 30's he wears a tweed jacket and is sporting late 70's apparel. He walks in to the static shot of the Damocles foundation, turns and addresses the camera.*

          PROFESSOR DAMOCLES
    Welcome to the Damocles Foundation,
    a place where you can come to rest.

EXT. DAMOCLES FOUNDATION - TV INFOMERCIAL

PATIENT'77A *stands with* **NURSE '77** *by the duck pond throwing pieces of bread in to the birds. Another patient sits on the bench reading a book Professor Damocles enters frame left, again to address camera.*

          PROFESSOR DAMOCLES
    Here you can spend that quality
    time YOU need, for as long as you
    want. Our staff are a dedicated
    team whose goal is to help you.

                                  CUT TO:

INT. WARD - TV INFOMERCIAL

PATIENT '77B *and* **ORDERLY '77** *chatting together over a game of chess or cards. The camera pans to Patient '77A who is sitting in a chair with Nurse '77 sitting on his lap, she is being slightly affectionate with him, and his face signifies that he is putting on a happy look (throw away plot device).*

> **PROFESSOR DAMOCLES**
> When you feel that the whole world
> is on your shoulders, we at the
> Damocles foundation are here to
> lift that burden.

                                    DISSOLVE:

Using video interference as a style

EXT. THE DAMOCLES FOUNDATION - MONDAY MORNING

Establishing shot showing the Foundation and the foreground sign, on which it states

> The Damocles Foundation
>
> Rehabilitating mental health sufferers since 1977

                                    CUT TO:

EXT. OFFICE - MONDAY MORNING

Close up on the name on the door

> Barker MD

                                CROSS FADE TO:

INT. OFFICE - MONDAY MORNING

ALICE *(Late Teens and with a bandage on her arm with a 'cant be arsed attitude')is sitting with their back to the camera, sitting next to her is a* **SOCIAL WORKER** *(business type, very stern)* **BARKER** *(Late 30's early 40's superior Business type) sits in her chair looking at a file.*

                                    CUT TO:

ALICE POV - MONDAY MORNING

She looks as Barker, who has a file in her hand, she opens it and turns the pages until she finds the right page. She picks up a pen and places it in front of Alice who signs the paperwork

                SOCIAL WORKER
     Just to Clarify, what exactly
     does this entail?

                  BARKER
     All that signing this form does
     is state that you are agreeing
     to be a guest here at Damocles,
     now that IS voluntary, you are
     welcome to leave at any time,
     but your pyrotechnic fantasies
     will only land you in further
     trouble. Here we help you
     before you get in to such a
     predicament a pre-emptive
     strike as it were. Especially
     with no next of kin or friends
     to speak of, it does look to me
     that we are your best option in
     to rejoining society as a
     valued citizen.

Alice hands back the pen and signed form,

                  BARKER
     See, nothing to it. I'm sure
     you'll fit in fine here,
     there are so many programs
     available for your
     rehabilitation.
        (she motions with her hand)
     Please.

CARPENTER *an attractive blonde security guard in her mid twenties steps forward and smiles at Alice.*

CARPENTER
Its OK you can trust me.

FADE TO BLACK

EXT. GRAVEYARD - DAY

GEORGE *(A scruffy man in his mid to late 20's) enters frame carrying a flower. Close in on (fake) gravestone (mum and Dad), George places the flower down by the grave.*

GEORGE
I'll make you proud of me, I've got an interview next week. Its as a janitor but at least it'll pay for the computer course. Since the lay off its been hard to get back in the game but I'm on my way.

He bows his head says a silent prayer, kisses his hand and touches the stone then stands and walks off camera right as he goes the camera pans with him but is unable to catch up as it passes a gravestone with the names of Alice's parents and sister on it.

Flash edits with news reports and footage of fire telling the story of Alice's life as a pyromaniac setting fire to her home in a suicide attempt where she survives and everyone else dies.

                    NEWSREPORTER Y2K
          Alice showed no remorse in
          court today as the 16 year old
          smirked as the ruling unfolded.

                       NEIGHBOUR
          This kid is (beep) up there's
          no hope for someone like that,
          lock the psycho up and throw
          away the key.

                    NEWSREPORTER Y2K
          As Alice Nochneya starts what
          will be a long term of
          incarceration.

Alice is behind bars looking up at camera
Reverse POV
A guard stands looking though bars, he looks down at her a smile on his face.

                        GUARD
          You belong to us now, the world
          will forget you ever existed.

INT. CORRIDOR - MONDAY MORNING

GEORGE is cleaning the corridor with a mop and bucket. On his uniform is a name badge, he is busy cleaning when he notices that the room to his left is now empty, he stops mopping and looks inside the room.

                                                    CUT TO:

INT. CORRIDOR - MONDAY MORNING

Close up of Carpenter her finger along the wall as she walks towards camera.

CUT TO:

Close up as George goes to open the door but Carpenter's hand grabs the door handle first preventing him from doing so.

CARPENTER
Working overtime are we?

GEORGE
Erm, yeah well thought I'd just, you know check on things before I left.

He looks in to the room.
POV George looking at SARAH who is sleeping in her room.

INT. CORRIDOR - MONDAY MORNING

George is looking in to the room while standing next to Carpenter, he looks uneasy standing next to the guard and so goes on his way. Carpenter watches him go then turns to the door and goes inside.

INT MONITOR - MONDAY MORNING

Looking at Sarah's room Carpenter closes the door and locks it. She tiptoes and pulls a cable out from the CCTV camera rendering it as static the Saffron Damocles an unseen mastermind taps the screen.

SAFFRON DAMOCLES
HMMMmmm

CUT TO:

INT. SARAH'S ROOM - MONDAY MORNING

Carpenter is standing above the sleeping patient, Carpenter loosens her collar and reaches forward as Sarah's eye opens for a shock factor, Carpenter pulls back the bed sheets.

> FADE TO BLACK:

INT. CORRIDOR - MONDAY MORNING

Outside Sarah's room as Carpenter exits the patients room nursing a bruised eye. Close up of Carpenter.

CARPENTER
(under her breath)
Fucking bitch!

INT. MONITOR - MONDAY MORNING

Carpenter walks down the corridor, she stops at a notice board and takes a pen from her top pocket close up as on the notice board we see the Stress therapy clipboard. She lifts the first two or three pages and then looks at the timetable on the sheet, she scribbles her name down in a free slot.

INT. MONITOR ROOM

Passage of time sequence using CCTV camera footage.

CCTV FOOTAGE - MONDAY EVENING

George is wandering down a corridor Slow pan of George with his back to the camera as Hooper steps up behind him.

CUT TO:

INT. ROOM - MONDAY EVENING

looking out as HOOPER an orderly appears behind the inquisitive George who jumps.

                HOOPER
Hey buddy, how's your first week been?

                GEORGE
Yeah not too bad so far, long days but I'll get used to it... erm, what happened to Sarah?

                HOOPER
Who?
   (slight pause to think)
Oh er yeah right, she was er transferred.

                GEORGE
Oh, she never said anything,
   (He looks back at Hooper)
we were supposed to play Mario Kart!
   (Holding up his Nintendo DS)
where did she go?

                HOOPER
Who knows pal, I just work here

He pats him on the shoulder and walks off.

CUT TO:

INT. CORRIDOR - MONDAY EVENING

George is skulking around looking at doors.

CUT TO:

Close up of well polished work boots walking towards the camera.

CUT TO:

George pauses outside the door of one of the patients, he looks inside and sees Barker tending to Alice.

INT. ROOM - MONDAY EVENING

looking out at George as he looks away and carries on walking.

CUT TO:

INT. BASEMENT - MONDAY EVENING

A box is tossed in to the fireplace. On the box is written.

    Sarah Dawson: Personal artefacts.

The box slowly burns in a drawn out sequence. The screen turns to static as if the channel has been turned.

TITLE SEQUENCE

Video footage
Professor Damocles addressing the camera in a tight framing

PROFESSOR DAMOCLES

> Observation is the key to understanding any mental illness, in order to heal we must first understand and to understand we must pay attention to the minutia.

We are now looking at CCTV footage within the Foundation, the screen changes from camera view to camera view, each one showing a different part of the Foundation. Important that the following scenes appear on the screen.

Hands on a vision mixer as buttons are pressed and dials are turned.
The operator is smoking and has a full ashtray on the console.
Passage of time sequence set around the location.

EXT. DAMOCLES FOUNDATION

Passage of time piece to indicate morning.

INT. ALICE'S ROOM - FRIDAY AFTERNOON

PROFESSOR DAMOCLES
(on TV)
Human nature instils an urge for personal space. Observing the patient in their safety zone gives the subject a feeling of safety.

Alice extreme close up of her eye as she wakes in her room, she looks bewildered. She looks around the room.

CUT TO:

Alice POV as she clears her focus on her surroundings George is emptying the bedside bin. Her focus clarifies.

Cut back to

3rd person camera

                    ALICE
    Who are you?

                    GEORGE
    I'm sorry luv, I didn't mean to
    wake you, I'll be going in a
    sec, go back to sleep, sorry.

                    ALICE
    No its OK, I just... who are you
    again?

                    GEORGE
    Sorry,

He places the small bin bag in a larger one then removes his gloves and moves closer.

                    GEORGE
    I'm George, the new dogsbody
    around this place
       (Nervous Chuckles)

                    ALICE
    I haven't seen you before.

                    GEORGE
    Yeah I've only been here a week

                    ALICE
    What happened to Billy?

GEORGE
Erm, I think she said he
transferred to another facility.

ALICE
(rolling her eyes)
Right.

Insert flashback scene

*Hooper (with his back to the camera) stands
watching the janitor (Billy) empty trash cans at
the back of the building Camera rushes towards
Billy as Hooper grabs him from behind
strangling / suffocating him with a plastic bag.*

HOOPER
You fucked her didn't you? Admit
it you fuck!

BILLY
(Struggling to make himself heard)
W---who

HOOPER
(Grinding his teeth in anger)
You fucking know who you cunt!,
you've been fucking my wife.

BILLY
I-ii-i i don't know what you're
talking about I don't even know
your wife.

*Cut this sentence off with Hooper stabbing his
head with a screw driver.*

HOOPER

Don't bullshit me you cock I know
what's been going on!
(he realises Billy is dead)
Fuck you!

*He lets go of the body and it drops to the floor.
Hooper POV looking down at body.*

HOOPER

CUNT!

He kicks the body.

Cut back to:

George, now standing next to Alice, looking down at her

GEORGE

Do you know what happened to
Sarah in the room next door? Do
you know where she was
transferred to?

ALICE

(Pause)
I wouldn't believe everything
you hear in this place

George, sits next to her, she moves her head to look at him.

ALICE

I swear this place got a lottery
grant but they definitely haven't
put the money into looking after us
that's for sure.

GEORGE
What do you mean?

He moves the chair and sits down next to her

ALICE
Just...

The door opens and in steps Carpenter

CARPENTER
Hey man.

George spins his head round With George in the extreme foreground and Carpenter in the background(focus).

CARPENTER
(Scowling)
Can you deal with the mess in 12, fucking twat just pissed all over the floor.

George gets up out of his chair.
Alice touches his hand and they exchange a glance. George looks a bit confused then picks up his stuff and exits the room.

Carpenter doesn't move out of the way as George squeezes past and out of the door. Staying on a static shot of Carpenter she stares at her for what seems like a long time then steps back and shuts the door.

INT. BASEMENT

Sarah is chained to the wall in a crucifix position close up on her chained wrists as we see the name Sarah stencilled on her wristband, she is very dirty, wounds are on her face and about her torso, the gown she is wearing is torn in places.

She is crying but as she is gagged her screams are somewhat muffled.

Pull back and switch focus to a close up of a knife being sharpened on a stone, this is a drawn out scene as the knife needs are tendered to.

The knife is lovingly put down on a small cloth. A small distance from the cloth sits a dated MiniDV hand held video camera on a small desk tripod. A hand enters the frame and turns the camera on, the flipped out screen flashes blue and then the image appears on the screen. The image shows Sarah she is out of focus. The hand adjusts the image making it sharp.

> FADE TO BLACK:

INT. DAYROOM - SATURDAY - MORNING

> **PROFESSOR DAMOCLES**
> (On TV)
> Communal areas allow for
> interaction and lead to social
> progress.

Extreme close up on a draughts board as a winning move takes place.

Camera pans up to reveal PATIENT Q excited about the win, reverse shot to show BLUTO who is upset about loosing, slamming their fist down on the table in anger.

Cut to:

PATIENT F at a different table looks up suddenly as he is shocked from the outburst, looking down at his drawing he has noticed he has gone outside the lines and is not happy, he screws up the drawing and crosses his arms in disgust, then begins to draw on a new piece of paper.

Sitting next to Patient F is Alice, she gets up and walks across the room as the camera follows her. She passes a chair on which is STABBY JOE he is watching Animal Soup on the screen in particular the face removing scene near the end of the film, he is laughing to himself. Alice moves over to the window and opens the blinds to look out at the pond/lake etc.

The opening of the blinds has caused the sun to enter the room and cast a light over the television set distorting Stabby Joe's view of the film. He frowns, looks at the TV then to Alice and back again, he calmly raises his foot up on to the chair and pulls up his trouser leg to reveal a nasty looking shank.

Nurse A crosses the frame carrying a tray with pills on it Stabby Joe calmly stands up.

CUT TO BLACK:

ALL PATIENTS
(off screen screaming)

CUT TO:

INT. BARKER'S OFFICE - SUNDAY NOON

Insert professor Damocles part here close up of a monitor on the screen is BARKER talking with ALICE

> **BARKER**
> So, Alice, how have you been these last few days. A lot has happened since you came here...
> (Pause as she checks)
> Not even 2 months now isn't it?
> Would you care to elaborate

> **ALICE**
> No

> **BARKER**
> Is that so? Well I guess I have to respect your decision. However I AM here to help you, to help you rehabilitate yourself and be suitable to return to society, so, is there anything that i can do to help you achieve your goals?

> **ALICE**
> (slow look up then raises head to eye level)
> Whatever I have to say you are going to dislike it anyway so I'm going to save us all the time and not bother.

BARKER
Now is that really the attitude
Alice. If you want to open up,
here and now IS the time.

*Barker leans forward looking in to Alice's eyes,
she then sits back and closes the file.*

BARKER
There is no judge and jury here
I just want to hear your views.
I am here to help YOU.

*An exchange of looks take place between the two
as Alice lowers her defences just a little*

ALICE
it's been hard for me here, I
don't belong here, I realized
yesterday that I...

Before she can continue Barker cuts in

BARKER
Yes lets talk about yesterdays
events in the day-room.

*Barker, bringing her offensive nature back in to
gear, begins to tap her ballpoint pen on the
table, this draws Alice's attention. Then Barker
raises the pen to her mouth and begins to nibble
the end. This makes Alice frown.*

ALICE
(in a stern voice)
That wasn't my fault. That
fuck-wit tried to stick me.

BARKER
Why did he want to do that? Did you provoke him? Did you say something to him?

ALICE
Don't try and push all the blame on to me, I'm the victim. He's a fucking prick who tried to stab me because he's fucking nuts, maybe the devil told him to do it or Jodie Foster, who the fuck knows alright,

BARKER
Now hold on a moment there, lets not forget why it is you are a guest here in this fine establishment.

ALICE
OK so I burn stuff, that's a little different from the amateur voodoo hour that was being held in the day-room yesterday. Why are you not having this conversation with him, why am I the one stuck in here listening to your sodding bullshit!

BARKER
loose the attitude Missy, whatever the case maybe, if there is an altercation between you and another guest, you must let us deal with it, you do not take it upon yourself to start chewing his face off!

INT. DAY-ROOM - SATURDAY - MORNING - FLASHBACK

Extreme close ups and jerky footage as STABBY JOE lifts his shank in a threatening manner, Alice leaps at him in defence and then sinks her teeth into his cheek. A GUARD grabs her.

INT. BARKER'S OFFICE - SUNDAY - AFTERNOON

Alice lets out a sly smile

      BARKER
  Now, lets look at the facts.
   (female guard hands her
   another file)
  Since you came here you have
  not exactly tried to adjust
  your behaviour. Let me remind
  you there is no one on the
  outside for you, you came here
  because this was your last
  chance, without us there is
  nothing for you, so why don't
  you grow up and let us help
  you. Firstly I want you to stop
  all these lies alienating you
  from the other guests and what
  is all this about accusing the
  staff of making inappropriate
  motions towards you?

INT. CORRIDOR - SUNDAY - AFTERNOON

George is listening on the other side of the door

      GEORGE
   (quietly to himself)
  Something ain't right here. I
  promise you, I'll expose it all

INT. BARKER'S OFFICE - SUNDAY - AFTERNOON

                      BARKER
All this bad behaviour and lies and what with yesterday do you honestly believe that I should allow this hearing to go through?
I got news for you sweetheart, you really need to buck up your ideas or you are going to be here a very long time.

Alice lowers her head but her eyes look around searching for something.

                      BARKER
In fact I am going to increase your medication and security over the next few weeks or until I start to see some improvement. I'm even going to recommend you partake in extra activities.

Alice's expression changes from smug to worried. Barker makes a note in the file Alice looks up at her again and then spits. The spit lands on the file and the Barker looks down at it.

                      BARKER
Thank you,
   (Alice looks confused)
You have just made it that much easier for me to sign your transfer papers. I've done all I can with you , perhaps you can find what your looking for elsewhere.

She wipes the file and picks up a stamp, slamming it on the paper it reads TRANSFER *in red text, she then closes the file.*

INT. CORRIDOR - SUNDAY - AFTERNOON

George moves along sweeping.

INT. MONITOR SUNDAY - AFTERNOON

Alice throws her seat back, the guard leaps in to action and manhandles Alice to the ground.

       GUARD
 Don't resist me you bitch.

          CUT TO:

STATIC FUZZ

          CUT TO:

INT. MONITOR - MORNING

Show the monitor as the subject we are following is George.

On the screen George is snooping, he looks through Sarah's empty room, in the drawers and in the closets, he then leaves the room.

Close up of a button being pressed

Back looking at the screen as George walks down the corridor, the camera following him switching to other cameras as and when necessary.

George tries the door for the records room, it is locked, he reaches for his keys but none of them fit the lock.

Watching the monitor as George sneakily hangs around the room as the camera zooms in on him.

                SAFFRON DAMOCLES
        (to herself)
      What are you up to Mr?

INT MONITOR - MORNING

As George bends down and tries to pick the lock.

                SAFFRON DAMOCLES
        (to herself)
      You really should mind your own business now shouldn't ya.

Insert close up of a hand picking up a radio and raising it out of shot.

                                    CUT TO:

INT. SMOKING AREA - MORNING

                   CARPENTER
        (Holding her radio to her mouth)
      Received, will check it out

She extinguishes her cigarette and exits frame left. The controllers hand moves to pick up a pen and then writes on a post-it-note.

The note reads

        Set up George's TRANSFER.

Transfer is underlined twice

INT. LOCKER ROOM - SUNDAY - NIGHT

Carpenter enters frame right taking off her jacket. The camera follows her to her locker. Opening the locker she places her jacket inside. Sitting on the bench and looking blankly into the adjacent locker is Hooper.

                    CARPENTER
        Hey man, how ya doin'

                    HOOPER
        Shagged out mate.

                    CARPENTER
        Look at it this way buddy, it's
        Wednesday soon, you know what that
        means.

Carpenter pulls off her t-shirt and grabs a body spray out of the locker. Hooper tosses a packet of pro plus into his locker and looks up at his colleague.

                    HOOPER
        Four days off.

                    CARPENTER
        Come on man, sound a little bit
        more enthusiastic.

She puts on a clean shirt and takes her work belt out of the locker and fastens it around her waist.

                    HOOPER
        Yeah but, I dunno, things with
        Susanne ain't the best at the
        moment so...

CARPENTER
Really? I thought things were fine.

HOOPER
I got a feeling she's been seeing someone else!

CARPENTER
Really?

HOOPER
Yeah, I cant prove it but its just something she said the other day.

CARPENTER
  (Putting her hand on his shoulder)
I'm sorry dude.

HOOPER
I might be wrong ya know.

CARPENTER
Yeah but dude, it's not as if you have remained monogamous have ya?

HOOPER
Yeah but...

CARPENTER
No buts... you cant really expect to live by the fact its one rule for you one rule for her now can ya.

HOOPER
I guess so but its still hard.

CARPENTER

Fuck off you poof. Imagine how she would feel if she knew you like I do.

HOOPER
(angrily)
She never will tho.. right?

CARPENTER

Hey, my lips are sealed...
(Touching his shoulder as she bends to do up her laces)
for the right price that is haha.

HOOPER
(Glancing at her crotch)
Yeah I bet, you'd open those lips for a fuckin' fiver you hoe.

Standing and tucking in his shirt

CARPENTER

Oi, you cheeky fucker, you've never had to pay me yet have ya?

HOOPER

Haha, right you ready.

CARPENTER
(Under her breath)
Maybe I'll bill ya.

HOOPER

Wha?

CARPENTER

Yep I'm ready, lets do it.

INT. CORRIDOR - SUNDAY – NIGHT

Hooper and carpenter make their way down the corridor, Hooper has a clipboard in his hand and is looking at the list of tasks.

    CARPENTER
 (looking over Hooper's shoulder)
Another transfer tonight I see.

    HOOPER
 (Looking down the page)
yeah,

    CARPENTER
Who is it this time?

    HOOPER
er
 (he looks at the sheet again)
Nochneya, Alice Nochneya

    CARPENTER
oh yeah she's that tasty bit of eurotrash in 7 who punched me in the fuckin eye.

    HOOPER
There may be a couple of nurses on but might just be quicker to move her ourselves right?

    CARPENTER
Shame, she did have a cracking arse on her, would've loved to have a pop at her myself.

HOOPER
Jeez, you'd fuck anything wouldn't ya?

CARPENTER
Well if it feels good do it I always say.

HOOPER
How is the husband then?

CARPENTER
Dave? He's OK I guess. Haven't seen much of him since he had to take on that second job... Christ, I swear I'm gonna have to have a go on euro millions this week, did ya see the prize was up to 46 million last week, fucking joke right.

INT. CORRIDOR - SUNDAY- NIGHT

Low shot of Hooper and Carpenter's legs as they approach the camera, there is little light.

INT. RECORDS ROOM - SUNDAY - NIGHT

George is rummaging through the filing cabinets looking for something with little success. His torchlight illuminating the folders in the filing cabinet as he thumbs through them.

INT. CORRIDOR - SUNDAY - NIGHT

HOOPER
I wouldn't know what to do with it!

CARPENTER
Could live off the interest
alone for the rest of me life
on a remote island.

HOOPER
Yeah I bet, having ya toes sucked
by an army of greasy cabana boys.

Show the door of the records room and pan down to the floor.

A flash light is moving within.

They pass the records room.

INT. RECORDS ROOM SUNDAY – NIGHT

George hears them outside and quickly turns off the light and ducks behind the desk. Close up of his eyes as he looks from right to left as the two walk past the office.

GEORGE
(Sigh of relief)

INT. CORRIDOR - SUNDAY – NIGHT

The two walk away from the camera and around a corner.

CUT TO:

The door of the office as George looks out at them, he then returns inside and closes the door.

INT. ALICE'S ROOM - SUNDAY - NIGHT

Alice wakes and in POV she looks at her feet, entering the room is an out of focus figure followed another. She is then wheeled out of her room and watching the ceiling as we pass strip bulb after strip bulb then enter an elevator.

INT. ELEVATOR - SUNDAY - NIGHT

Watch as the numbers descend.

INT. CORRIDOR - SUNDAY - NIGHT

George exits the records room with a series of papers in his hand, he stuffs them in his shirt and closes the door behind him. He looks to the right then to the left, he then exits screen right.

INT. ELEVATOR - SUNDAY - NIGHT

Alice being wheeled out of the elevator and into the basement.

                                                Cut to static fuzz

INT. TV
A dated newsroom

> **NEWSREPORTER CIRCA 1985**
> Today in a tragic turn of events at the Damocles Foundation, a patient attacked and killed the facility founders wife. Onlookers were so shocked at the speed and outright violence and rage within the patient that many of them were unwilling to comment on the incident. Sasha Damocles was declared dead on arrival by paramedics, her husband and child are reported to be seeking solitude in the family mansion and are planning on leaving for New York after the funeral to be held this Weekend, Professor Damocles sent us this statement

Cut to a video feed from within the mansion

> **PROFESSOR DAMOCLES**
> I am deeply distraught be the fact that someone i was trying to help lashed out and retaliated in such a way that left my daughter Saffron without a mother and me a widower. We can see that violence and aggression occur in a complex dynamic that in this instance was escalated by an unforeseen trigger mechanism, I will not let this turn of event interrupt my goal, in fact this is an instigator for what is to become a far more concentrated mission.

FADE TO BLACK:

INT. STAFF ROOM

Hooper is dialling a number on the staff pay-phone.

INT. HOME

SUSANNE *picks up phone, she is sitting in a cushion filled couch wearing comfy slacks we have the impression she has skipped work.*

                      SUSANNE
    Hello.

INT. STAFF ROOM

                      HOOPER
    Hey hon its me, I got your
    text, what's up?

INT. HOME

Her face drops as she prepares herself for the serious conversation that is to follow

                      SUSANNE
    Yeah right, I've been thinking
    and I thought it might be
    better if you move out for a
    while, I think we need the
    space right now.

                      HOOPER
      (V.O.)
  wha?

SUSANNE
Just for a while you know.

INT. STAFF ROOM

SUSANNE
(V.O.)
What with everything that's going on I just thought...

Hooper, leans back and looks up at the ceiling, his hand drops slightly so the receiver is no longer directly to his ear, his eyes begin to gain rage then he sighs and raises the receiver.

SUSANNE
(V.O.)
...that it would be easier on us both you know.

HOOPER
But hon, I don't want to be away from you, cant we work it out.

SUSANNE
(V.O.)
I'm sorry, I've made my mind up on this, I've been speaking with my mum,

Hooper groans

SUSANNE
(V.O.)
She's gonna come over later and stay here.

HOOPER
Well where the hell am I supposed to go?

INT. HOME

                SUSANNE
I'm sorry, I've made my mind up.

INT. STAFF ROOM

                HOOPER
For fuck sake, you keep doing this to me.

                SUSANNE
  (V.O.)
Hang on, fuck you, this has been a hard choice for me, I've been having all these mixed feelings and I wanted to do the right thing, this break might do us the world of good. I want to love you but I just feel we're moving apart.

                HOOPER
Moving apart, yeah you bet we are, it ain't your mum, is it, its that fucker you've been seeing.

                SUSANNE
Oh now you accuse me of cheating. You stupid prick, it took you long enough didn't it. I was gonna spare your feeling but nah fuck it.

                HOOPER
So you admit it then you whore!

SUSANNE
Hey, you brought that up and it's not exactly like you're a saint now is it. You and that little miss rotten crotch you work with, been bumping like rabbits.

HOOPER
Whatever!

SUSANNE
Really, great come back you fucking looser. I didn't want it this way but you ain't giving me much choice are ya.

He puts the phone down and thumps the wall. Hooper stands looking at the notice board. On which we see leaflets for certain items i.e. dog cage.

He focus' on the stress therapy timetable, seeing that carpenter has several sessions booked in.

He looks down and pulls out his wallet and looks at the picture of his pregnant girlfriend. He begins to look both sad and angry, he takes a deep breath, screws up the photo and throws it in the bin and puts wallet away and pulls a pen out of his pocket and runs the nib along the page looking for a vacant slot.

As he moves in to claim a spot, the focus shifts and barker appears in the background.

BARKER
Hey! You OK?

HOOPER
(slightly startled)
Erm yeah I was just... erm

BARKER
That's OK, you want to have a session do you?

HOOPER
I...

BARKER
It's OK, I understand. Everyone has a unique experience during this program, we can set something up solely to help you. It doesn't have to be like the last time if you don't want it to be.

Hooper looks over to her then back to the board and back again.

HOOPER
Last time did help but you're right, something more personal would be better.

Barker looks at her watch

BARKER
I got a few minutes, you wanna come in now and we can come up with something to ... suit your needs... promise I wont bite.

Hooper lets out a nervous smile and then follows her into the room and the door closes behind them.

INT. BASEMENT - MONDAY - EARLY

Static video feed with Professor Damocles talking about confinement and Proxemic preference

> title card:
> Monday November 1 2010 6:58am

                              FADE IN FROM
                              BLACK:

In ECU Alice's eyes open, she looks around the dark room.
Wider shot to reveal Alice's right hand is handcuffed above her to some pipes, as the camera pulls back we see we are in a dirty basement, littered with torture devices, a table with implements of nastiness.

There is a cage in the center of the room, inside which a figure sleeps (CHERYL).

The sound of off screen machinery fill the air. The shot consists of the corner of the cage and Alice in the back ground, some fingers are poking through the cage.

                    ALICE
        (She looks at her hand and tries to
        free it)
    Is there anyone there? HELLO?

The fingers in the cage twitch

                    ALICE
  HELLO?

CHERYL
Be quiet

Alice looks around quickly trying to see who had spoken to her.

ALICE
Who's there? Where am I?
What do you want from me?

CHERYL
(abruptly)
I said be quiet, If you make too
much noise they'll come in.

Cheryl shifts herself in her cage, she is wearing a hospital gown and is covered in oil, dirt, bruises and scars, she has a leg brace on her left leg and an eye patch over her right eye.

ALICE
Who are you, where are we

CHERYL
They'll come back if you
don't shut up.

ALICE
wha...

CHERYL
(whispering)
We're in the basement, they
brought me down here too and if
you don't piss em off you'll
stay alive.

STABBY JOE
(off camera SCREAMING)

Alice looks over to the door.

> **ALICE**
> Who was that?
>
> **CHERYL**
> It's another patient now
> shurrup or they'll hear you.
>
> **ALICE**
> Why are we down here, what's gonna
> happen to us?
>
> **CHERYL**
> shhh, play dead.
>
> **ALICE**
> wh...
>
> **CHERYL**
> Shut up and fucking do it OK.

Cheryl slumps down in her cage Hooper enters the room with two bowls of food in his hands, he moves over to the table and places the bowls down, he then takes just one bowl over to Cheryl and squats down, he looks deep in to her eyes and then passes the bowl in through the bars. He stands, steps out of frame, Cheryl ravenously leaps for the food and eats. The guard then re enters the frame now holding the other bowl, he bends down and drops to one knee near Alice, he moves her hair out of her eyes and she spits at him. He throws the bowl of food all over her.

> **BARKER**
> (over the tanoy)
> Would Guard Hooper please report to
> my office immediately.

Hooper groans and then gets to his feet and exits the room.

CUT TO BLACK:

INT. CORRIDOR - MONDAY - MORNING

Static fuzz cutting to video feed of Professor Damocles talking about personal space and the need for a safety zone where patients can make it their own without the risk of boundary violation The camera is pans up the stocking clad legs of NURSE Ratched and NURSE PRICE slowly as they stand outside a patients room.

      NURSE RATCHED
  Can you believe that guy last
  night?
      NURSE PRICE
  (she smirks)
I know, who the hell did he
think he was

      NURSE RATCHED
  Who in their right mind acts
  that way?

      NURSE PRICE
He probably belongs in here!

      NURSE RATCHED
  Or he bloody escaped from here
  we'll have to check the records
  for Tom and what was the other
  guy's name?

      NURSE PRICE
Dunno, began with an 'H' I think.

NURSE RATCHED
I know Halloween parties always bring out the crazies but they took the piss! That big guy was far too much in to his character.

NURSE PRICE
You're telling me, people like that shouldn't be allowed out
    (she laughs)
god knows what would've happened if we had gone back with them.

NURSE RATCHED
You slut, you wouldn't have would ya?

NURSE PRICE
Probably not but there was no one else worth shagging was there.

They come to a stop in front of a door

NURSE RATCHED
    (looking at her clipboard)
You wanna check out this next guy then!

NURSE PRICE
    (looking at her colleague inquisitively)
Oh yeah!

NURSE RATCHED
Hell yeah, such a shame he's catatonic.

CUT TO:

INT. ROOM - MONDAY - MORNING

The two nurses enter the room, inside is **SLOTH** *in bed, he is not moving at all but looking in to space.*

NURSE PRICE
(brushing his hair with her hand)
What happened to him.

Nurse Ratched looking back now at the clipboard in her hand, she lifts the first page, looking at the second.

NURSE RATCHED
Not a lot is known really, he was admitted yesterday in this catatonic state, no family, no one really knows who he is, his personal effects give us no leads, bit of a loner by all accounts, shame really.

NURSE PRICE
What are we supposed to do to help him, I mean if he's non responsive and all.

NURSE RATCHED
Not much we can do really, just wash him look after him for the night, he's being placed in this 'Transfer Program' tomorrow.

NURSE PRICE
Transfer program?

NURSE RATCHED
Yeah you know, the
(makes quotation marks in the air)
transfer program, he's a prime
candidate now, he's got no one
just a shame he's brain dead
and unresponsive, a bit of a
waste if ya ask me but someone
will have fun with him.

Nurse Price lifts his gown.

NURSE PRICE
(under her breath)
I'd Fuck his brains out first.

Nurse Ratched frowns and looks over to Nurse Price having heard her comment

NURSE RATCHED
If you think you can get a 'rise'
out of our new friend Sloth here
then, be my guest.

NURSE PRICE
I'll take that challenge.

CUT TO:

Close in on Sloth's eyes, they are dead and looking straight up beyond the camera position.

CUT TO:

INT. CORRIDOR - MONDAY - MORNING

SKITTLES (a 'geezer' patient) *is wandering unsupervised in the corridor he wanders up to a room window and peers in.*

CUT TO:

INT. ROOM - MONDAY - MORNING

Skittles POV

The 2 nurses molest Sloth who is blissfully unaware of the goings on Nurse Price moves over to the bed. She then turns her back on the man and hoists up her skirt then leans on to the back of the chair allowing him to see her arse. She then reaches under her skirt and with a seductive wiggle manages to remove her underwear, she takes them fully off, catching them on her heel as she does so then moves the undergarments gently over his face.

CCTV Footage of this event

INT. CORRIDOR - MONDAY - MORNING

Guard Carpenter is walking down the corridor escorting a patient (Bluto) ,coming the other way is Hooper

                HOOPER
    (Looking at Bluto)
Where are you taking this ... thing?
              CARPENTER
Yeah, can ya believe it, third time this week he's got out
    (Under her breath)
Fucking mongoloid
    (Normal volume)
Anyway, what you been up to then?

              HOOPER
    (sheepishly)
Huh

                    CARPENTER
             You, what you done now?

Hooper looks blankly at her.

                    CARPENTER
             What you done to get summoned by
             little miss all high and mighty

Hooper shrugs.

                    CARPENTER
             oh well, good luck whatever it is

Carpenter begins to walk away and as she does so she taps Hooper's shoulder in way to suggest good luck Hooper looks down to the ground and then walks on the camera follows Hooper's feet as he steps into a mop. He and the camera look up at George.

                    GEORGE
             Oops sorry pal

Hooper tilts his head in a way to suggest 'whatever' takes a slight pause as he notices some pages stuffed in Georges shirt, he looks back up at Georges eyes and then continues on his way. George stops mopping and leans on his mop watching.

Hooper walks away and as he goes he radios a message to someone.

INT. OFFICE - MONDAY - MORNING

From the POV of the CCTV a knock at the door is heard. Barker is sitting at her desk, she turns in her chair and is now facing the door.

BARKER

It's open

the door creaks open

CUT TO:

Behind Hooper as he pushes open the door in the background.

Barker sits behind her desk the focus shifts to the nurse as she stands and circles her desk until she is at the front of it, she leans back.

BARKER

You took your time, is everything OK?

HOOPER

(nodding)
uhuh.

BARKER

How are you feeling since your phone call?

HOOPER

To be honest our last session was great but...

BARKER

But what?

HOOPER

I feel a bit guilty.

BARKER

Now is a bit late to have a conscious call don't cha think.

Hooper lowers his head as he thinks for a second or two

BARKER

You are bigger than this. She's the past. You need to concentrate on the present
   (hoisting herself on to the desk,)
and look to the future.

HOOPER

I guess.

BARKER

Well, I told you it'll be fine. I'm just glad I can help in your progress. Do you need to book in any more session?

HOOPER

um, yes, this is definitely working for me.

BARKER

Come, sit down.

Hooper, shot from behind Barker, walks in and sits down. The camera follows his movement so as he sits the camera shows that his face is in line with her crotch. Barker opens her legs and his eyebrows raise before he nervously looks up at her.

INT. CORRIDOR

CCTV footage as Carpenter walks down the corridor,

                                                  CUT TO:

Follow her feet as she unlocks a door with a

restricted access

sign on it. She enters and closes the door behind her.

INT. DARKENED ROOM

There is only one light coming from the room, a television screen showing static sits in a rack underneath is a video cassette player, its time has not been set and is therefore flashing 00:00. In close up, Carpenter's hands place a video cassette into the machine and press the play button.

INT. TV

Close in on the screen as it changes from static to a clip of the basement with Sarah chained in a crucifix position, the shot starts out of focus but then slowly becomes a sharp image. A figure enters the frame and unlocks the chains holding Sarah in place, as she is unlocked, she slumps down.

VIDEO CARPENTER
(very quiet)
Sit up straight.

Sarah looking very distraught sits upright, the camera image shifts focus again to compensate.

INT. DARKENED ROOM

Carpenter adjusts the volume then turns to camera

CARPENTER
There you go sweetheart, now trust me, you're gonna love this.

Zoom out with Carpenter as she moves to a couch, the camera moves over the couch and comes to a halt, a girl is sitting on the couch.

VIDEO CARPENTER
Take off all your clothes!

Real Carpenter sits down and looks to the girl sitting next to her.

INT. TV

Sarah is now very distraught, she is reluctant to look at the camera.

VIDEO CARPENTER
Now take your shirt off
 (she ignores the voice)
NOW!

She jumps in terror and then proceeds to take her shirt off but doing it so that she keeps her breasts covered to the best of her ability throughout, on her left breast is a distinctive tattoo of the ace of spades. In to the shot enters a knife, the tip of the knife is running over her hand trying to pry away the fingers.

VIDEO CARPENTER
I wanna see ... you

Sarah starts to cry as the knife begins to pull her hand away from her breast.

INT. DARKENED ROOM

Cut to face on of Carpenter as she looks at the screen enthralled, she then looks down at her crotch then looks over to her companion.
Quick cuts (fixed cam) speed up the sequence so it becomes clearer what is on her mind, inter cut TV images of Sarah's breasts.

Carpenter takes her hand and shoves it down her trousers.

On the screen the knife is toying with the nipple, flash cut with Carpenter putting her head back in excitement, cut with the hand down her trousers and her head back with her eyes rolling.

                    CARPENTER
          (Under her breath passionately)
        Oh shit.

INT. TV

Screen shows Sarah being stabbed to death.

INT. DARKENED ROOM

                    CARPENTER
          (Orgasming)
        Fuck yeah.

INT. TV

screen focuses on Sarah's face as the life drains from her then after a while cuts to static.

INT. DARKENED ROOM

BIG REVEAL as we see that the companion on the couch is a naked Sarah she has wounds over her body and we can see the tattoo again. Carpenter goes up to the TV, and presses stop she then moves back to the girl. Staying on the static TV

FADE TO BLACK:

INT. BASEMENT - MONDAY - NOON

Hooper enters the room with a box, Alice looks intrigued, she then sees the label Patient ID # 6918GJ Alice Personal effects.

ALICE
Hey that....

Hooper turns to her and frowns, She sinks back down, his eyes burning in to her for several moments before he returns his attention to the box in front of him. Alice continues to watch with great interest as he opens up the sealed box and rummages through the items. He takes particular interest in the contents pocketing those that he wants (he finds her underwear sniffs it and places them in his pocket). He looks back at Alice and taps his ass like the ASDA adverts. He then throws the remaining items in a bag labelled for incineration only.

STABBY JOE
(off camera)
screaming

Hooper mumbles in disgust then leaves the room.

CHERYL
I'm sorry!

ALICE
What?

CHERYL
Your times up hon!

Alice looks both worried and confused.

CHERYL
I'm afraid I've seen it all before
(Under her breath)
Far too many times.

ALICE
What? What do you mean 'times up'?

CHERYL
You've been transferred.

ALICE
Huh?

CHERYL
They've filed you as being transferred all they need to do now is clear up the loose ends

ALICE
What loose ends?

CHERYL
(after a slight pause)
You!

Alice immediately starts to try and free herself from the handcuff but only succeeds in cutting her wrists more and more so she slumps down crying.

She then looks up to see Cheryl is watching her intently then looks from her hand to the door and back again as off camera the sounds of screaming heighten her urge to break free.

She struggles so much that her wrist begins to bleed.

CHERYL
It's no use you know

Alice slumps down and looks over to Cheryl

CHERYL
It's best if you don't escape, they'll only find you and when they do you'll pray for a quick death believe me.

ALICE
Fuck off! How can you just sit here, if they wanna kill me they're gonna have to be ready to die as well!

CHERYL
Seriously, if you run, it'll be a bad choice.

ALICE
How long have you been here, haven't you tried to get out, what do they want from us?

CHERYL
You have no idea what is going on
here, YES I have tried to escape,
 (beat)
twice in fact.
 (beat)
Those fuckers found me
 (beat)
both times.

Cheryl looks off camera in the direction of Stabby Joe's screams, close in on her eyes.

CLEVER DISSOLVE:

FLASHBACK SEPT 30TH 2010 THURSDAY

Black screen

CHERYL
(VO)
I had been down here for days, I
didn't know exactly how many.

FADE IN:

Close up of Cheryl crouched in a corner she has a rope tied to her ankle and to a pipe on the wall, she has managed to loosen the knot enough to free her foot, she struggles with it and it cuts in to her skin as she removes it.

CHERYL
(VO)
This had become my tomb, no
windows, only one way in and out. I
was alone, I only saw them when
they bothered to feed me, but then
they brought in someone else.

A light breaks across her face as the door of the basement is opened, in comes Hooper dragging Sarah. He cuffs her to the overhead piping then tosses her clothes in the furnace.

CHERYL
(VO)
At the time I owed my life to her as she offered me the distraction I needed to escape. I will never forget her face as she looked at me.

Sarah looks at the camera, tears rolling down her cheek as Cheryl pauses and then ducks out the door.

CHERYL
(VO)
I should have tried to save her.

Low angle following Cheryl as she runs blindly down a corridor into a distant light. Cheryl has pushed open a hole in the wall, she squints at the bright light from the daylight. She begins to pull herself through. In the background she can hear Hooper screaming.

HOOPER
(off camera at distance)
Get back here you fucking cunt!.

Cheryl keeps checking behind her as she squeezes through the window.

POV HOOPER

As he sees the lower half of Cheryl stuck Winnie-the-pooh style in the gap in the wall. He slowly moves up to her then his hand reaches out and runs up her leg in an almost sensual way, close up of his face as he looks at the leg lovingly and with great interest.

EXT. WINDOW

She stops and begins to scream, then almost jolts backwards as she is obviously pulled by Hooper.

POV HOOPER

In the room, Hooper has his hand tight around her calf muscle. He then brings a crowbar straight down into the back of her kneecap dislocating it instantly. She screams in agony.

CUT TO:

INT. TORTURE ROOM - PRESENT - MONDAY - AFTERNOON

          CHERYL
They brought me back here, I never saw the girl again. They kept me well fed to start with and looked after me really well. I thought I would be able to get away again as soon as they turned their backs.

Cut in close up of Alice listening.

          CHERYL
I cant even remember how I got out the second time, the tunnels are like a maze.

EXT. WOODS - DUSK - FLASHBACK 2 OCT 16TH 2010 SATURDAY

                    CHERYL
     (VO)
     God only knows how I made it
     outside.

Cheryl now wearing the leg brace is running through the woods, constantly looking back over her shoulder, she is very dirty and her gown is torn.
Cut in close ups of Carpenter's feet running after her.
This scene to be shot continuously and at a distance Cheryl is grabbed and she stumbles to the ground and Carpenter is on top of her.

                    CARPENTER
     Don't ever run from me you little
     whore.

Carpenter reaches for her hunting knife and slices at her face across her eye then slams the knife down in to the ground next to her head she's so scared she freezes and looks terrified. Hooper begins to kick her Carpenter gets off her and they both kick her.

                    CHERYL
     (VO)
     I don't really know what happened
     next, I was in a bad way. I don't
     even know how I got back here.

INT. BASEMENT - PRESENT - MONDAY - AFTERNOON

CHERYL
I woke in this cage and I've been here ever since.

ALICE
(slight pause)
My god, I cant believe it, how long have you been in there.

CHERYL
(pause)
Too long.

ALICE
We got to get out of here. You need to get this out and expose those sick fuckers. This place, these people. It HAS to STOP!

CHERYL
I've tried, its no use, they'll never give up, they will hunt you down and kill you.

ALICE
Well I ain't just gonna sit here. We are getting the fuck outta here right now.

Alice starts to pull at her wrist and frantically looking for something to aide in her escape, even spitting at it to aide lubrication, She fiddles with the handcuff lock but to no avail, she begins to cry and slumps down exhausted.

Slow track back

FADE TO BLACK:

INT. DAYROOM - MONDAY - AFTERNOON

Nurse Ratched puts gloves on to tend to Patient 13, in the background George is sweeping the floor but listening to the conversation.

> **NURSE RATCHED**
> (Applying blood pressure strap)
> So how have you been, settling in OK?

> **PATIENT 13**
> (looking at her arm)
> Yes, I think so, haven't really made any friends tho.

> **NURSE RATCHED**
> Well, I know that the guards have developed their own stress therapy activities that are apparently very beneficial for them, kind of an army thing, you know break em down to rebuild em. I have had a few ideas along the same sort of thing to help rehabilitate the guests maybe you'll like to take part. I have to go now but just call me if you want anything.

The camera dollies around the nurse.

CUT TO BLACK:

INT. BOX - MONDAY - AFTERNOON

BLACK
The noise of people moving around is overpowered by the noise of a man heavy breathing followed by the sounds of his pounding on the box he is trapped within.

>   **STABBY JOE**
> Let me out of here!

>   **NURSE RATCHED**
>   (quietly)
> Shurrrup!

The shot shows a beam of light enter the box, then we follow it to the hole.

EXT. BOX - MONDAY - AFTERNOON

Looking in at the eye.

INT. BOX - MONDAY - AFTERNOON

Reverse shot of his POV looking out at the nurse sharpening a knife.

>   **STABBY JOE**
> let me out you cunt!

the Nurse puts the knife sharpener back on the table with a thud, she sighs and storms over to the box and pounds on the top the sound is very loud. His cries turn to whimpers as she continues to watch out of the box. The body of the Sarah is wheeled in and Nurse Ratched goes to her bag of tools (chisels etc.). She begins to chop up the body. Nurse Ratched cuts off a body part and throws it for Cerberus the Dog to eat.

                    NURSE RATCHED
            I'm almost done here then we can
            get a shifty on with Stabby Joe
            over there.

She motions with her saw towards the box and walks out of shot.

                                        CUT TO BLACK:

Suddenly Nurse Ratched looks directly into the box, eye to eye in a sudden shock moment Stabby Joe falls back. Suddenly a crowbar is pounded in to the top of the box, then again and again and again then a slight light pierced through the shot again it is pounded. Show her levering the top off the crate.

INT. BOX - MONDAY - AFTERNOON

The light fills the shot and there sits the man. He has a bloody plaster on his cheek, he is squinting from the light as the shot bleaches out to white.

INT. OFFICE - MONDAY - LATE AFTERNOON

The door creaks open and sneakily, George enters the room. He looks around the room then catches sight of the Laptop. He removes the pages from his shirt and moves over to the desk and sits in the chair.

Constantly checking the door with his eyes in case someone is coming he begins to search the computer. He searches for patient names followed by looking for transfer records.

After a lengthy scene (pc graphics) we discover the familiarities with each patient. Words stand out over others.

It dawns upon him He reaches for his keys, on which is a USB data pen, he plugs it in to the laptop and begins copying files. While the data transfer is in progress he notices a CCTV icon on the screen and double clicks on it.

Looking for the corridor cam he stumbles across other screens that are inappropriate. He comes across the basement camera up on the screen comes the text - Access denied other user logged on. He looks confused and annoyed. He sees the archive section and in that computer folder are the names of the missing patients. He double clicks on one again he is blocked by a password prompt.

GEORGE

Bollocks

CUT TO:

INT. MONITOR ROOM

Saffron Damocles is watching the feed from the office as George uses the laptop.

CUT TO:

INT. OFFICE - MONDAY -LATE AFTERNOON

George continues to check the feeds, at the bottom of the feed is a line of text indicating the room number, he goes back to the hidden feed he moves the mouse and sees a tab labelled captures, clicking it he is shocked to see that the captured frames are that of Alice in the

basement. He stands back quickly shocked at what he sees. Then He looks closer at the image, at the top of which is a room reference.
He shuts everything down removes his USB pen then moves for the door.

INT. CORRIDOR - MONDAY - LATE AFTERNOON

He passes the notice board, next to which is the map of the foundation, he takes a double look and then examines it, seeing where he is now and looking for the room reference he sees that it is out the back of the grounds.

CUT TO:

Monitor showing Carpenter walking down a corridor.

CUT TO:

EXT. FOUNDATION GROUNDS

George runs from the foundation building to the secondary exit. Montage scene quick cuts to show the emergency.

EXT. BASEMENT - MONDAY - LATE AFTERNOON

George tries the door CCTV footage of him entering the basement CCTV footage of Carpenter moving faster down the corridor but always missing his head out of shot.

INT. BASEMENT - MONDAY - LATE AFTERNOON

Alice looks abruptly to Cam L Cheryl looks abruptly to Cam R George's feet descend the steps Alice looks at her restraints and again tries to free herself.

EXT. SECONDARY ENTRANCE

George gets up to the padlocked door on which is a restricted access sign. He picks up a brick and smashes the lock The Door suddenly opens (colour change from red to green).

UNKNOWN POV - MONDAY - LATE AFTERNOON

Looking at George fiddling with his keys, George looks up a look of terror on his face.
A hand lashes out and slices George's neck with a scalpel, the movement of the cut makes George spin allowing him to spray blood over the walls, his body falls to the ground and spasms violently as his life drains from his body.
Carpenters feet enter behind the body.

FADE TO BLACK:

INT. BASEMENT - MONDAY - EARLY EVENING

Carpenter enters the room dragging the body of George in with her.
She drags the body through the room and past the two girls.
Alice watches as she goes past, terror fills her eyes at the sight of the body. As Carpenter then walks back and out of the room she watches her feet spread bloody footprints across the floor.

EXT SMOKING AREA - MONDAY - EARLY EVENING

Carpenter opens a door and enters the smoking area, Hooper is already there.

NURSE RATCHED
Give us a fag mate.

HOOPER
Hard day?

NURSE RATCHED
Unexpected lets put it that way

HOOPER
(handing her a cigarette)
I hear that.

Hooper points at her shirt

HOOPER
Nose bleed?

NURSE RATCHED
(Looking down at the blood on her shirt)
Shit! Yeah something like that

She leans back to the wall taking a puff of her cigarette.
Slow zoom in to her face as she looks into space.
Hooper goes to say something but doesn't.
Long pause.

NURSE PRICE
At least this stress therapy is free right?

HOOPER
Yeah but I sometimes think about the consequences.

NURSE RATCHED
Yeah well, what happens at work stays at work right?

He nods as does Nurse Price in agreement and goes to take a drag of her cigarette

HOOPER
Surely if we continue we'll get caught tho right?

NURSE RATCHED
Bollocks! That's the whole benefit of No next of kin. Barker sure does pick em well.

HOOPER
I guess so. But sooner or later...

NURSE RATCHED
Look! Its all cool, I just sorted out a loose end and I'm sure she'll fix that if not those above have the skill.

HOOPER
Yeah that's true, 's not as if I got anything to loose any more.

NURSE PRICE
Yeah how is the slag?

HOOPER
Fuck her man, she'll get what's coming to her.

Nurse Ratched nods, while he looks menacingly in to space.

>   **HOOPER**
>   (Under his breath)
>   Hell yeah, she'll get it soon
>   enough.
>   **CARPENTER**
>   Whoa, whatever killer haha
>   (then looking over to nurse Price)
>   How's your day been?
>
>   **NURSE PRICE**
>   Ha, you know same shit different
>   day really.
>
>   **HOOPER**
>   (Snapping out of his moment)
>   Ha, yeah, hey tell her about that
>   fella in room 6?
>
>   **NURSE PRICE**
>   Oh hell yeah check this out right,
>   so we'd been messing around with
>   this catatonic guy right and I'm
>   standing there OK holding his ...

The scene looses sound as we

                                        CUT TO:

EXT. SMOKING AREA - MONDAY - EARLY EVENING
CCTV footage as Nurse Price demonstrates the goings on with the catatonic guy, she is highly animated and making very obscene hand gestures as Hooper and Ratched both fall about laughing. Hooper leaves the area back through the doorway leaving the two alone.

THE ESCAPE - MONDAY - EARLY DUSK

Alice, Biting down on her gown to stop herself from screaming, pulls back hard on her thumb, dislocating it with a loud pop and crunch

ALICE
FUCK!!!!

CHERYL
I warned you! They will hear you. Now we're all fucked.

ALICE
(out of breath)
Bollocks, I don't care, I'm getting out of here now.

CHERYL
They always know.
(Quietly)
Its like they are watching.

Alice pulls her hand free from the cuff, the pain getting more intense as she looks very pale and almost gags on vomit. The clasp slips off her hand.

ALICE
(swearing in her native tongue)

Close up of Cheryl's eyes as she frowns in displeasure.

Alice tries to get to her feet but stumbles a little from both the exhaustion and the pain, she cradles her hand as she gets to her feet and looks around the room.

Seeing the dead body of George she reaches down and relieves him of a wrench, she then turns back to the cage and slams it into the locking mechanism.

With every slam, Alice and Cheryl look in the direction of the door. Alice drops the wrench in the haste of the moment, she goes to grab it but Cheryl's hand beats her to it! Cheryl thumps Alice in the face flooring her.

Cheryl gets out and straddles her grabbing her hair and thumping her head against the floor two or three times.

ALICE
What the fuck are you doin? Get the fuck offa me.

CHERYL
You must not leave. You have to stay here with us.

ALICE
(Struggling to talk)
Wha...

CHERYL
Stay here with me...
...and the others

ALICE
fuck off, you crazy bitch, what's your problem God dammit

CHERYL
You are mine... I chose you

ALICE

What?!

CHERYL

The day you came here i wanted you to be my first.

ALICE

You sick fucker what the hell...

CHERYL
(Cutting her off)
I wanted to break you. I saw how strong willed you were.

Alice embraces an overdose of adrenaline and they both roll to the side allowing Alice to get on top.

ALICE

Happy to disappoint you, you stupid cunt!

She punches Cheryl in the face but with her damaged hand. The pain is almost too much and Alice leans over herself in agony. In an instant Cheryl picks up the wrench and brings it slamming into Alice's upper arm, Alice falls off of her but manages to stay on her feet and makes for the door.

INT. THE BOUDOIR

Alice bursts into a room, almost falling to her feet she gathers herself and stands up but then almost throws up from the smell of rotting flesh, she scans the room. The candle lit room is littered with numerous dead women's bodies and several skeletons.

In the one corner of the room Hooper sits in a chair, in his arms is the dead body of Susanne, he is looking sorrowful a tear rolling down his blood spayed face. He looks up at Alice.

HOOPER
It wasn't my fault, she made me do it.

Alice looks shocked and her eyes are darting from left to right.

HOOPER
I asked her to be reasonable but she kept screaming at me.

Alice notices a crib, surrounded by candles. She nervously steps towards the crib, hoping there is no baby there but she sees movement under the ragged cloth, afraid for the child she moves more towards it Hooper lifts his hand, in which is hand gun, she gasps and stops in her tracks. He waves the gun around willy nilly.

HOOPER
She just kept screaming and screaming.

He points the gun at Alice.

HOOPER
You won't leave me will you?

ALICE
Er, no of course not...
  (Pause)
... in fact I was just looking for you. I thought we could go and feed the ducks.

He looks at her then he looks down at his dead ex girlfriend.
Insert flash edits of Hooper killing Susanne he begins to silently cry, his hand against his head still holding the gun, he points it at Alice.

HOOPER
No, you hate me!

ALICE
No I don't, I...

Hooper stands up leaving Susanne on the ground, he steps towards Alice. He grabs her with his left hand she struggles and lashes out then goes still when he brings in the gun he hovers it over her eye for a second or two then cracks a disturbing smile and moves the gun under his chin and pulls the trigger.

Alice covers her mouth in shock and jumps back a little.

She moves closer to the body and then moves towards the crib and covers her mouth as she steps even close but she is determined to save the child. She gets nearer and nearer. Shot from within the crib Alice gets right up and enters focus as she reaches in, pauses to look behind her as a steps are heard, she returns her focus to the baby and reaches in.

ALICE
Sssh its OK sweetheart

Shot from above the blanket is pulled back to reveal a dead baby and a live rat.

Alice stammers back in both shock and disgust and slips on spilled guts of a dead nurse laying there half naked with a dead foetus in front of her on the floor.

Hearing the steps getting louder Alice slips and slides as she gets to her feet and makes her way to the far door.

As she gets there she stops and looks back at the horrific sight of corpses and incineration bags. Scanning for anything useful. She sees a gas canister then the furnace. She turns on the furnace.

Lifting up her gown she pulls down the top of her waistband of her panties to reveal a match and lights the furnace.

As she goes to exit she grabs the cannister and twists the nozzle then legs it out of the room.

EXT. SECONDARY EXIT

Alice runs round from the corner alerting Carpenter and Cerberus who are patrolling the grounds then.

KABOOM!

An explosion erupts from undergrounds obliterating the secondary exit as Alice throws herself to the ground.

Cerberus and Carpenter see the explosion, Cerberus runs away, Carpenter falls to her rear end, she is close to Alice who on all fours pushes herself up and runs fro Carpenter picking a brick off the ground in the process, leaping on top of Carpenter.

POV Carpenter as Alice brings the brick down to her face repeatedly.

CUT TO:

Special effect shot of face head mashed up with wig as in a side view and over the top gore hungry close ups as Alice smashes the brick into the face head of carpenter. Shoot in slow motion as she continues to pound the face in to the ground, track back.

EXT. WOODS - MONDAY - EARLY DUSK

Alice runs into focus and stops to catch her breath at a tree, she looks up and can see the road not far beyond the trees.

EXT. COUNTRY ROAD - EARLY DUSK

A car is travelling down a single lane country road.

INT. THE CAR - EARLY DUSK

The Stereo plays A music Track while **HOT GIRL** *drives and* **DOUCHEBAG** *sits in the passenger seat*

      DOUCHEBAG
Are you sure this is a short cut?

                        HOT GIRL
            Trust me OK if we'd stayed on
            the dual carriage way, we'd be
            stuck in traffic and we'd never
            make it in time. At least this
            way we're still moving closer.

EXT. WOODS - EARLY DUSK

Alice runs she is panting heavily as she is
getting more and more tired.
                                            CUT TO:

EXT. COUNTRY ROAD - EARLY DUSK

Close ups of the car wheel turning.
                                            CUT TO:

EXT. WOODS - EARLY DUSK

Alice getting closer and closer to the road

INT. WOODS - MONDAY - EARLY DUSK

*Alice begins to run for the road, she looks back
behind her as she can hear noises but continues
to run flat out. She is getting scratched by
branches and falls a few times before clambering
up the side of the road and manages to get on to
the tarmac.*

EXT. WOODS / ROAD - MONDAY - EARLY DUSK

*Alice steps in to the road and tries to flag down
a car, but it zooms passed just as she steps on
to the tarmac as the car disappears from site
around a bend, her posture slumps as she gets
disheartened. Wide shot Alice in the middle of
the road looking at the car.*

INT. CAR - MONDAY - EARLY DUSK

      DOUCHEBAG
  We're lost just admit it

Douche-bag leans forward and starts to fiddle with the stereo infuriating Hot Girl to the point where we can see her temper is about to erupt. He flicks a switch and a really lame pop track comes on and his face lights up just as her hand enters the shot slapping him across the face.

      BLAMMO

The car hits Alice obliterating her body with an eruption of blood and gore.

Inside the car the two of them scream with a red glow from the blood on the windscreen.

The burned arm (all that remains of Alice) lands in the bushes.

Cut to the car now crashed in to a tree as inside Hot Girl is dead over the wheel and Douche-bag is impaled by an object.
          CUT TO BLACK:

TV

      NEWSREPORTER Y2K
  In a strange turn of events today
  the prestigious Damocles Foundation
  was destroyed in an arson attack by
  one of the very patients the
  foundation was trying to help. Our
  memories are returned to 1985 when
  a patient at the foundation struck
  out killing the founders wife.

NEWSCASTER CIRCA Y2K Cont.

This time the patient was a known arsonist who had only been at the facility for a short time, she herself was also found dead outside the grounds where she had been hit by vehicle while trying to flee the scene. Amongst the dead are countless brilliant minds in the medical profession. A dark day for medicine that has been felt around the world.

NEWSROOM NEWS CASTER

Miss Saffron Damocles the director of the Damocles Foundation having taken over the helm after her fathers untimely death in 1999 had this to say.

NEW YORK

SAFFRON DAMOCLES

Today is a very sad day for us all I'm glad my father isn't here to see this as it was his goal to help people despite a similar turn of events resulting ion my mothers death he always strived to see the best in people and help them to live out to there full potential.
At our facility here in New York we will hold a minute silence in honour of those who fell in today's tragedy.

Pull out from television to a static shot from behind as The Monitor aka Saffron Damocles looks out the window, due to the lighting she is cast in shadow her mobile phone rings cutting to a medium shot Left side view as she pulls the phone out of her right pocket and up to her right ear.

SAFFRON DAMOCLES

Speak.

MR YAKOMOTO

(VO)
Sorry to bother you miss but we have encountered a few problems here at the foundation

SAFFRON DAMOCLES

Problems? Please, enlighten me.

MR YAKOMOTO

(VO)
We've had an unexpected backfire on one of our test candidates. It's resulted in my having to transfer some respected employees.

SAFFRON DAMOCLES

(Abruptly)
Well I must admit I find this most unsatisfactory, I have been counting on your success. My grandfather hand picked you for your creativity and determination but here we are with you trying to blame failure on to those under your instruction. This is a blatant lack of managerial duties.

SAFFRON DAMOCLES Cont.

If you cannot live up to the expectations of our founder, god rest his sole, then surely you are about as much use as a one legged man in an arse kicking contest. Now get this sorted, I want to see positive results by the end of the month and I want you to clear up all this mess.

MR YAKOMOTO
(VO)
Yes miss I wont let you down again

SAFFRON DAMOCLES
Well I should hope not. Especially with this shambles in the UK. I want all privileges to your test subjects removed immediately, the less they hear about what happens in the real world the better, isolate all candidates to solitary confinement within the hour and cancel all interactions in the day room I do not want my fathers hard work pissed away in an instant.

MR YAKOMOTO
I-iii-

SAFFRON DAMOCLES
Get it done. Good bye.

She terminates the call (close up of button press) sitting at her desk she grabs the mouse insert computer graphics #7.
Close up of her hands on the keyboard spelling out

Terminate Transfers and Initiate
re-assignment program.
Subject 0001 Tomagashii Yakomoto. Japan facility

Fade to Black:

Roll Credits.

Made in the USA
Charleston, SC
19 April 2016